50 Persian Lunch Recipes for Home

By: Kelly Johnson

Table of Contents

- Fesenjan (Pomegranate Walnut Stew)
- Zereshk Polo (Barberry Rice)
- Ghormeh Sabzi (Herb Stew)
- Tahchin (Saffron Rice Cake)
- Khoresh-e Bademjan (Eggplant Stew)
- Baghali Polo (Fava Bean Rice)
- Kotlet (Persian Meat Patties)
- Ash-e Reshteh (Noodle Soup)
- Sabzi Polo Mahi (Herb Rice with Fish)
- Gheimeh (Split Pea and Meat Stew)
- Adas Polo (Lentil Rice)
- Dolmeh Barg (Stuffed Grape Leaves)
- Kookoo Sabzi (Herb Omelette)
- Baghali Ghatogh (Fava Bean and Dill Stew)
- Polo Zereshk-o Morgh (Barberry Chicken Rice)
- Asheh Mast (Yogurt Soup)
- Mirza Ghasemi (Eggplant and Tomato Dip)
- Lubia Polo (Green Bean Rice)
- Joojeh Kabab (Chicken Kebabs)
- Kalam Polo (Cabbage Rice)
- Shirin Polo (Sweet Rice)
- Morasa Polo (Jeweled Rice)
- Mast-o Khiar (Cucumber Yogurt)
- Loobia Polo (Persian Rice with Green Beans)
- Zeytoon Parvardeh (Marinated Olives)
- Asheh Reshteh (Noodle and Herb Soup)
- Koofteh Berenji (Rice Meatballs)
- Shirazi Salad (Cucumber Tomato Salad)
- Baghali Polo Ba Mahicheh (Dill and Lima Bean Rice with Lamb)
- Abgoosht (Persian Meat Soup)
- Kufteh Tabrizi (Tabriz-style Meatballs)
- Maast-o Esfenaj (Yogurt and Spinach Dip)
- Dizi (Persian Lamb Stew)
- Sheer Khurma (Milk and Date Pudding)
- Faloodeh Shirazi (Rosewater Sorbet)

- Khoresh-e Karafs (Celery Stew)
- Morgh Polo (Chicken Rice)
- Mast-o Khiar Ba Mosamma (Cucumber Yogurt with Mint)
- Gondi (Chickpea and Chicken Dumplings)
- Baghali Polo Ba Morgh (Dill and Lima Bean Rice with Chicken)
- Tahdig (Crispy Rice)
- Khoresh-e Gheymeh Bademjan (Eggplant and Meat Stew)
- Havij Polo (Carrot Rice)
- Koofteh Sabzi (Herb Meatballs)
- Khoresht-e Beh (Quince Stew)
- Zaban (Persian Beef Tongue Stew)
- Sholeh Zard (Saffron Rice Pudding)
- Kalam Polo Ba Morgh (Cabbage Rice with Chicken)
- Gondi Polo (Chickpea and Chicken Rice)
- Reshteh Polo (Rice with Noodles and Herbs)

Fesenjan (Pomegranate Walnut Stew)

Ingredients:

- 1 cup walnuts, finely ground
- 1 large onion, finely chopped
- 2 tablespoons vegetable oil
- 500g chicken, cut into pieces
- 1 cup pomegranate molasses
- 1 tablespoon sugar (optional)
- Salt and pepper to taste

Instructions:

In a large pot, sauté the chopped onions in vegetable oil until golden brown.
Add the chicken pieces to the pot and brown them on all sides.
Stir in the ground walnuts and continue cooking for a few minutes until the walnuts release their oils.
Pour in the pomegranate molasses, add sugar (if desired), and season with salt and pepper.
Bring the mixture to a simmer, then reduce the heat to low, cover the pot, and let it simmer gently for about 1-1.5 hours until the chicken is tender and the stew has thickened.
Taste and adjust the seasoning, adding more salt, pepper, or sugar if needed.
Serve the Fesenjan over rice, and enjoy this delightful Persian dish!

Zereshk Polo (Barberry Rice)

Ingredients:

- 2 cups Basmati rice
- 1 cup barberries (zereshk), washed and drained
- 1/2 cup sugar
- 4 tablespoons butter
- 1/4 teaspoon saffron threads (optional)
- 2 tablespoons hot water (for saffron, if using)
- Salt, to taste

Instructions:

Rinse the Basmati rice under cold water until the water runs clear. Soak the rice in water with some salt for about 30 minutes.

In a pot, bring water to a boil. Drain the soaked rice and add it to the boiling water. Cook until the rice is parboiled, about 6-8 minutes. Drain the rice.

In a separate pot, melt 2 tablespoons of butter. Add a thin layer of parboiled rice to the pot, then add a layer of barberries and sprinkle with sugar. Repeat the layers until all rice and barberries are used.

Create holes in the rice using the back of a wooden spoon handle to allow steam to escape. Place small pieces of butter on top.

Dissolve saffron threads in hot water if using, and drizzle over the rice. This step adds a beautiful color and flavor.

Cover the pot with a clean kitchen towel and put the lid on top. Cook on low heat for about 45-50 minutes or until the rice is fully cooked and fluffy.

Once done, gently mix the rice and barberries together.

Serve Zereshk Polo on a platter, and enjoy this delicious and visually appealing Persian dish!

Ghormeh Sabzi (Herb Stew)

Ingredients:

- 1 cup chopped parsley
- 1 cup chopped cilantro
- 1/2 cup chopped fresh fenugreek leaves (or dried fenugreek leaves)
- 1/2 cup chopped green onions
- 1 cup chopped chives
- 1 large onion, finely chopped
- 3 tablespoons vegetable oil
- 500g stewing beef or lamb, cubed
- 2 dried limes (limoo amani), pierced
- 1 teaspoon turmeric
- 1 teaspoon ground black pepper
- Salt, to taste
- 1 cup red kidney beans (canned or pre-cooked)
- 1 tablespoon dried fenugreek (if not using fresh)
- 2 tablespoons lemon juice (optional)

Instructions:

In a large pot, sauté the chopped onions in vegetable oil until golden brown.
Add the cubed meat to the pot and brown it on all sides.
Stir in the chopped herbs (parsley, cilantro, fenugreek leaves, green onions, and chives) and continue cooking until the herbs are wilted.
Add turmeric, black pepper, and salt to the pot. Mix well to combine.
Add dried limes to the pot, and pour enough water to cover the ingredients. Bring it to a boil.
Reduce the heat to low, cover the pot, and let it simmer for about 2-3 hours until the meat is tender.
If using dried fenugreek, add it to the stew at this point.
Add the pre-cooked or canned red kidney beans to the stew and continue simmering for an additional 30 minutes.
Adjust the seasoning, and if desired, add lemon juice for a hint of acidity.
Serve Ghormeh Sabzi over rice and enjoy this flavorful Persian herb stew!

Tahchin (Saffron Rice Cake)

Ingredients:

- 2 cups Basmati rice
- 3 cups plain yogurt
- 3 eggs
- 1/2 cup vegetable oil
- 1 teaspoon ground saffron threads, dissolved in 2 tablespoons hot water
- Salt, to taste
- 1/2 teaspoon black pepper
- 1 tablespoon melted butter or oil for greasing the baking dish

Instructions:

Rinse the Basmati rice under cold water until the water runs clear. Soak the rice in water with some salt for about 2 hours.
In a large pot, bring water to a boil. Drain the soaked rice and add it to the boiling water. Cook until the rice is parboiled, about 6-8 minutes. Drain the rice.
In a bowl, beat the eggs and mix them with yogurt, vegetable oil, dissolved saffron, salt, and black pepper.
Add the parboiled rice to the yogurt mixture and mix well until the rice is fully coated.
Grease a round or rectangular baking dish with melted butter or oil. Pour the rice and yogurt mixture into the dish, spreading it evenly.
Cover the baking dish with aluminum foil and bake in a preheated oven at 350°F (180°C) for about 45-50 minutes, or until the edges are golden brown and a crust forms on top.
Once done, let it cool for a few minutes. To serve, invert the Tahchin onto a serving platter, revealing the golden crust.
Cut into wedges and serve warm. Tahchin can be enjoyed on its own or as a side dish.

Enjoy this delicious Persian Saffron Rice Cake!

Khoresh-e Bademjan (Eggplant Stew)

Ingredients:

- 2 large eggplants, peeled and sliced
- 1 large onion, finely chopped
- 500g stewing beef or lamb, cubed
- 3 tomatoes, peeled and chopped
- 2 tablespoons tomato paste
- 2 tablespoons vegetable oil
- 1 teaspoon turmeric
- 1 teaspoon ground cinnamon
- Salt and pepper, to taste
- 1 cup water
- 2 tablespoons lemon juice (optional)
- Fresh parsley for garnish

Instructions:

Heat vegetable oil in a pot and sauté the chopped onions until golden brown.
Add the cubed meat to the pot and brown it on all sides.
Stir in turmeric, ground cinnamon, salt, and pepper. Mix well to coat the meat with the spices.
Add chopped tomatoes and tomato paste to the pot. Cook for a few minutes until the tomatoes start to break down.
Pour in water, cover the pot, and let it simmer on low heat for about 1.5 to 2 hours until the meat is tender.
While the meat is simmering, prepare the eggplants. Heat oil in a separate pan and fry the eggplant slices until they are golden brown. Set aside on paper towels to absorb excess oil.
Once the meat is tender, add the fried eggplants to the stew. Gently mix them in, being careful not to break the eggplants.
If desired, add lemon juice for a hint of acidity. Adjust salt and pepper to taste.
Cover the pot and let it simmer for an additional 20-30 minutes until the flavors meld together.
Garnish with fresh parsley and serve Khoresh-e Bademjan over rice or with flatbread.

Enjoy this comforting and flavorful Persian Eggplant Stew!

Baghali Polo (Fava Bean Rice)

Ingredients:

- 2 cups Basmati rice
- 1 cup fresh or frozen fava beans, shelled
- 1/2 cup fresh dill, chopped
- 3 tablespoons vegetable oil
- 1 teaspoon ground saffron threads, dissolved in 2 tablespoons hot water
- Salt, to taste

Instructions:

Rinse the Basmati rice under cold water until the water runs clear. Soak the rice in water with some salt for about 2 hours.

In a large pot, bring water to a boil. Drain the soaked rice and add it to the boiling water. Cook until the rice is parboiled, about 6-8 minutes. Drain the rice.

In a separate pot, bring water to a boil and blanch the fava beans for 2-3 minutes. Drain and set aside.

In the same pot used for rice, add vegetable oil and a thin layer of parboiled rice. Then add a layer of fava beans and chopped dill. Repeat the layers until all rice and beans are used.

Pour the dissolved saffron over the top layer of rice and beans.

Create holes in the rice using the back of a wooden spoon handle to allow steam to escape.

Cover the pot with a clean kitchen towel and put the lid on top. Cook on low heat for about 45-50 minutes or until the rice is fully cooked and fluffy.

Once done, gently mix the rice, beans, and dill together.

Serve Baghali Polo on a platter, and enjoy this aromatic Persian dish!

Baghali Polo is often served with lamb or chicken, providing a delightful combination of flavors.

Kotlet (Persian Meat Patties)

Ingredients:

- 500g ground beef or a mixture of beef and lamb
- 2 large potatoes, boiled and mashed
- 1 large onion, grated
- 2 eggs
- 1/2 cup breadcrumbs
- 1 teaspoon turmeric
- Salt and pepper, to taste
- Vegetable oil for frying

Instructions:

In a large bowl, combine the ground meat, mashed potatoes, grated onion, eggs, breadcrumbs, turmeric, salt, and pepper. Mix the ingredients thoroughly until well combined.

Take a portion of the mixture and shape it into a round or oval patty. Repeat until all the mixture is used, creating patties of uniform size.

Heat vegetable oil in a frying pan over medium heat.

Fry the patties in the hot oil until they are golden brown on both sides, turning them as needed. This usually takes about 3-4 minutes per side.

Place the cooked kotlets on a plate lined with paper towels to absorb any excess oil.

Serve the kotlets warm with your favorite side dishes or in a sandwich.

Kotlet is often enjoyed with Persian flatbread, fresh herbs, and a squeeze of lemon. It can also be served with rice or as part of a sandwich with lavash or pita bread. Enjoy your delicious Persian meat patties!

Ash-e Reshteh (Noodle Soup)

Ingredients:

- 1 cup dried reshteh (Persian flat noodles) or linguine, broken into smaller pieces
- 1 cup cooked chickpeas
- 1 cup cooked red kidney beans
- 1 cup chopped fresh herbs (a mixture of parsley, cilantro, dill, and green onions)
- 1 large onion, finely chopped
- 3 cloves garlic, minced
- 2 tablespoons vegetable oil
- 1/2 cup kashk (Persian whey, or substitute with Greek yogurt)
- 8 cups chicken or vegetable broth
- 1 teaspoon turmeric
- Salt and pepper, to taste
- 2 tablespoons dried mint (for garnish)
- 2 tablespoons butter (optional, for garnish)

Instructions:

In a large pot, sauté the chopped onions in vegetable oil until golden brown.
Add minced garlic to the pot and sauté for an additional minute until fragrant.
Add turmeric, salt, and pepper to the pot. Mix well to combine.
Pour in the chicken or vegetable broth and bring it to a boil.
Add the broken reshteh (noodles) to the boiling broth and cook until they are tender, usually about 10-15 minutes.
Stir in the cooked chickpeas and red kidney beans.
Add the chopped fresh herbs to the pot, reserving some for garnish.
Once the soup is well-cooked and the flavors meld together, stir in kashk (or Greek yogurt) to add a creamy texture. Adjust the seasoning if needed.
In a separate pan, melt butter (if using) and add dried mint. Fry for a minute until the mint becomes fragrant.
Serve Ash-e Reshteh hot, garnished with a drizzle of minted butter and a sprinkle of fresh herbs.

This Persian noodle soup is hearty and flavorful, perfect for a comforting meal. Enjoy!

Sabzi Polo Mahi (Herb Rice with Fish)

Ingredients:

- 2 cups Basmati rice
- 1 bunch fresh herbs (a mixture of parsley, cilantro, dill, and fenugreek), finely chopped
- 1 large onion, thinly sliced
- 4 fish fillets (such as white fish or trout)
- 1/2 cup vegetable oil
- 1 teaspoon ground saffron threads, dissolved in 2 tablespoons hot water
- Salt and pepper, to taste
- Lemon wedges for serving

Instructions:

Rinse the Basmati rice under cold water until the water runs clear. Soak the rice in water with some salt for about 2 hours.

In a large pot, bring water to a boil. Drain the soaked rice and add it to the boiling water. Cook until the rice is parboiled, about 6-8 minutes. Drain the rice.

In a pan, sauté the sliced onions in vegetable oil until they become golden brown. Add the finely chopped herbs to the sautéed onions and cook for a few minutes until the herbs are wilted.

In a separate pan, sear the fish fillets on both sides until they are cooked through. Season with salt and pepper.

Grease the bottom of a pot with a bit of oil. Place a layer of parboiled rice, followed by a layer of the herb and onion mixture, and then another layer of rice. Repeat until all the rice and herbs are used.

Drizzle the dissolved saffron over the top layer of rice.

Create holes in the rice using the back of a wooden spoon handle to allow steam to escape.

Cover the pot with a clean kitchen towel and put the lid on top. Cook on low heat for about 45-50 minutes or until the rice is fully cooked and fluffy.

Once done, gently mix the rice and herbs together.

Serve Sabzi Polo Mahi on a platter, placing the seared fish fillets on top. Garnish with lemon wedges.

Enjoy this delightful Persian dish of herb-infused rice with perfectly cooked fish!

Gheimeh (Split Pea and Meat Stew)

Ingredients:

- 1 cup yellow split peas, rinsed and soaked for 1-2 hours
- 500g stewing beef or lamb, cubed
- 1 large onion, finely chopped
- 2 tomatoes, peeled and chopped
- 2 tablespoons tomato paste
- 1/4 cup dried lime (limoo amani), pierced
- 2 tablespoons vegetable oil
- 1 teaspoon turmeric
- Salt and pepper, to taste
- 1 teaspoon ground cinnamon
- 1 tablespoon dried fenugreek leaves (optional)
- 2 tablespoons lemon juice (optional)
- 1 tablespoon sugar (optional)
- Fried potatoes for garnish (optional)

Instructions:

In a pot, heat vegetable oil over medium heat. Sauté the chopped onions until golden brown.
Add the cubed meat to the pot and brown it on all sides.
Stir in turmeric, ground cinnamon, salt, and pepper. Mix well to coat the meat with the spices.
Add chopped tomatoes and tomato paste to the pot. Cook for a few minutes until the tomatoes start to break down.
Drain the soaked split peas and add them to the pot.
Pour in enough water to cover the ingredients, add dried lime, and bring the mixture to a boil.
Reduce the heat to low, cover the pot, and let it simmer for about 1.5 to 2 hours until the meat is tender, and the split peas have softened.
If using, add dried fenugreek leaves to the stew.
Adjust the seasoning and add lemon juice or sugar if desired, depending on your taste preferences.
Optionally, fry thinly sliced potatoes until golden brown and use them as a garnish.
Serve Gheimeh over rice and enjoy this flavorful Persian split pea and meat stew!

This dish is often served with rice and can be accompanied by torshi (Persian pickles) or a side salad.

Adas Polo (Lentil Rice)

Ingredients:

- 2 cups Basmati rice
- 1 cup brown or green lentils, rinsed
- 1 large onion, finely chopped
- 2 tablespoons vegetable oil
- 1 teaspoon ground cumin
- 1 teaspoon ground cinnamon
- Salt and pepper, to taste
- 2 tablespoons raisins (optional)
- 2 tablespoons slivered almonds or chopped pistachios for garnish
- Saffron threads, dissolved in hot water (optional, for color)

Instructions:

Rinse the Basmati rice under cold water until the water runs clear. Soak the rice in water with some salt for about 2 hours.

In a large pot, bring water to a boil. Drain the soaked rice and add it to the boiling water. Cook until the rice is parboiled, about 6-8 minutes. Drain the rice.

In a separate pot, heat vegetable oil over medium heat. Sauté the chopped onions until they become golden brown.

Add the rinsed lentils to the sautéed onions and cook for a few minutes until they start to soften.

Add ground cumin, ground cinnamon, salt, and pepper to the lentils and onions. Mix well to combine.

In the same pot, layer the parboiled rice and lentil mixture. Repeat until all the rice and lentils are used.

Optionally, add raisins between the layers for sweetness.

Drizzle saffron water over the top layer of rice for color.

Create holes in the rice using the back of a wooden spoon handle to allow steam to escape.

Cover the pot with a clean kitchen towel and put the lid on top. Cook on low heat for about 45-50 minutes or until the rice is fully cooked and fluffy.

Once done, gently mix the rice and lentils together.

Serve Adas Polo on a platter, garnished with slivered almonds or chopped pistachios.

Enjoy this flavorful and nutritious Persian lentil rice as a main dish or as a side!

Dolmeh Barg (Stuffed Grape Leaves)

Ingredients:

- Grape leaves (fresh or jarred, about 40-50 leaves)
- 1 cup Basmati rice, rinsed
- 300g ground beef or lamb
- 1 large onion, finely chopped
- 2 tablespoons vegetable oil
- 1/4 cup tomato paste
- 1/4 cup dried tamarind paste (or lemon juice as a substitute)
- 1 teaspoon ground cinnamon
- 1 teaspoon ground allspice
- Salt and pepper, to taste
- 2 tablespoons chopped fresh mint
- 2 tablespoons chopped fresh dill
- 2 tablespoons chopped fresh parsley
- 1/2 cup pine nuts (optional)
- 2 cups water

Instructions:

If using jarred grape leaves, rinse them under cold water to remove excess brine. If using fresh grape leaves, blanch them in boiling water for a few minutes until they are softened. Drain and set aside.

In a pan, sauté the chopped onions in vegetable oil until they become translucent. Add the ground meat to the pan and cook until browned. Drain any excess fat.

Stir in tomato paste, tamarind paste (or lemon juice), ground cinnamon, ground allspice, salt, and pepper. Mix well and cook for a few minutes until the flavors meld.

Add the rinsed Basmati rice to the meat mixture and continue cooking for another 5 minutes.

Remove the mixture from heat and let it cool slightly. Stir in chopped mint, dill, parsley, and pine nuts if using.

Take a grape leaf, shiny side down, and place a spoonful of the rice and meat mixture near the stem end.

Fold the sides of the leaf over the filling and roll tightly into a cylinder shape. Repeat the process until all the filling is used.

Line a pot with a layer of grape leaves, then arrange the stuffed grape leaves on top in layers.

Pour 2 cups of water over the stuffed grape leaves and place a plate on top to keep them from floating.

Cover the pot and cook on low heat for about 45-50 minutes or until the rice is fully cooked.

Let the Dolmeh Barg cool slightly before serving.

Enjoy these delicious Persian stuffed grape leaves as an appetizer or a main dish!

Kookoo Sabzi (Herb Omelette)

Ingredients:

- 2 cups chopped fresh herbs (a mixture of parsley, cilantro, dill, and chives)
- 6 large eggs
- 1 onion, finely chopped
- 1/2 cup walnuts, chopped (optional)
- 2 tablespoons dried barberries (optional)
- 1 teaspoon baking powder
- 1/2 teaspoon turmeric
- Salt and pepper, to taste
- 3 tablespoons vegetable oil

Instructions:

In a large bowl, beat the eggs until well combined.
Add chopped herbs, finely chopped onion, chopped walnuts (if using), dried barberries (if using), baking powder, turmeric, salt, and pepper to the beaten eggs. Mix everything together thoroughly.
In a non-stick frying pan, heat vegetable oil over medium heat.
Pour the herb and egg mixture into the pan, spreading it evenly.
Cook the Kookoo Sabzi over medium heat for about 15-20 minutes or until the edges are set and the bottom is golden brown.
Once the bottom is cooked, carefully flip the omelette using a plate or lid. Cook the other side for an additional 10-15 minutes until fully set and golden brown.
Once cooked through, transfer the Kookoo Sabzi to a serving plate.
Let it cool for a few minutes before slicing it into wedges.
Serve the Kookoo Sabzi warm or at room temperature.

This herb-filled omelette is a popular Persian dish, often served as a main course or sliced into smaller pieces and enjoyed as an appetizer. It can be served with flatbread, yogurt, or pickles on the side. Enjoy!

Baghali Ghatogh (Fava Bean and Dill Stew)

Ingredients:

- 2 cups frozen or fresh fava beans
- 1 cup chopped fresh dill
- 1 large onion, finely chopped
- 3 cloves garlic, minced
- 3 tablespoons vegetable oil
- 1 teaspoon turmeric
- 1 cup water
- 2 tablespoons rice flour (optional, for thickening)
- Salt and pepper, to taste
- 1 tablespoon dried fenugreek leaves (optional)
- 2 tablespoons lemon juice

Instructions:

If using fresh fava beans, shell them from the pods. If using frozen, thaw them.
In a pot, sauté the chopped onions in vegetable oil until golden brown.
Add minced garlic to the pot and sauté for an additional minute until fragrant.
Stir in turmeric, salt, and pepper. Mix well to combine.
Add fava beans to the pot and sauté for a few minutes.
Pour in water, cover the pot, and let it simmer on low heat for about 15-20 minutes or until the fava beans are tender.
In a small bowl, mix rice flour with a bit of water to create a smooth paste (if using). Add it to the stew to thicken it, stirring continuously to avoid lumps.
Stir in chopped fresh dill and dried fenugreek leaves (if using). Cook for an additional 5-10 minutes until the flavors meld together.
Add lemon juice to the stew and adjust the seasoning if needed.
Serve Baghali Ghatogh hot, preferably over rice.

This flavorful and aromatic Persian stew is a delightful way to enjoy fava beans and dill. It is often served as a main course, especially during the spring when fresh fava beans are in season. Enjoy!

Polo Zereshk-o Morgh (Barberry Chicken Rice)

Ingredients:

- 2 cups Basmati rice
- 500g chicken pieces (preferably bone-in, skin-on for added flavor)
- 1 large onion, thinly sliced
- 1 cup barberries (zereshk), washed and drained
- 4 tablespoons vegetable oil
- 1 teaspoon ground saffron threads, dissolved in 2 tablespoons hot water
- Salt and pepper, to taste

For Chicken Marinade:

- 1 cup plain yogurt
- 2 cloves garlic, minced
- 1 teaspoon ground cumin
- 1 teaspoon ground coriander
- Salt and pepper, to taste

Instructions:

Rinse the Basmati rice under cold water until the water runs clear. Soak the rice in water with some salt for about 2 hours.
In a bowl, mix together the yogurt, minced garlic, ground cumin, ground coriander, salt, and pepper for the chicken marinade.
Marinate the chicken pieces in the yogurt mixture for at least 1-2 hours or overnight in the refrigerator.
In a large pot, bring water to a boil. Drain the soaked rice and add it to the boiling water. Cook until the rice is parboiled, about 6-8 minutes. Drain the rice.
In a separate pot, heat 2 tablespoons of vegetable oil over medium heat. Sauté the sliced onions until golden brown.
Add marinated chicken pieces to the pot and brown them on all sides.
Stir in barberries and continue cooking for a few minutes until they soften.
In the same pot, layer the parboiled rice and the chicken and barberry mixture. Repeat until all the rice and chicken are used.
Drizzle saffron water over the top layer of rice.

Create holes in the rice using the back of a wooden spoon handle to allow steam to escape.

Cover the pot with a clean kitchen towel and put the lid on top. Cook on low heat for about 45-50 minutes or until the rice is fully cooked and fluffy.

Once done, gently mix the rice, chicken, and barberries together.

Serve Polo Zereshk-o Morgh on a platter, and enjoy this flavorful Persian dish!

This dish is often garnished with additional saffron-infused rice on top and can be served with a side of salad or yogurt. Enjoy!

Asheh Mast (Yogurt Soup)

Ingredients:

- 2 cups plain yogurt
- 1/4 cup rice, rinsed
- 1 cup chopped fresh herbs (a mixture of mint, dill, parsley, and chives)
- 1 large onion, finely chopped
- 2 cloves garlic, minced
- 2 tablespoons vegetable oil
- 4 cups water or chicken broth
- 1 tablespoon dried mint (for garnish)
- Salt and pepper, to taste

Instructions:

In a pot, heat vegetable oil over medium heat. Sauté the chopped onions until they become translucent.
Add minced garlic to the pot and sauté for an additional minute until fragrant.
Stir in the rice and continue cooking for another 2-3 minutes.
Pour in water or chicken broth and bring the mixture to a boil. Reduce the heat and let it simmer until the rice is fully cooked.
In a separate bowl, whisk the plain yogurt until smooth.
Gradually add a ladle of the hot broth to the yogurt, stirring continuously to avoid curdling.
Slowly pour the yogurt mixture back into the pot, stirring constantly.
Add chopped fresh herbs to the pot and season with salt and pepper. Simmer for an additional 10-15 minutes, stirring occasionally.
Adjust the seasoning if needed and ensure the soup is heated through.
In a small pan, fry dried mint in a bit of oil until it becomes fragrant.
Serve Asheh Mast hot, garnished with a drizzle of fried mint.

Enjoy this refreshing and tangy Persian yogurt soup as a light and comforting dish! It's often served with flatbread or as a starter to a larger meal.

Mirza Ghasemi (Eggplant and Tomato Dip)

Ingredients:

- 2 large eggplants
- 4 tomatoes, peeled and chopped
- 4 cloves garlic, minced
- 2 tablespoons vegetable oil
- 3 eggs
- 1 teaspoon ground turmeric
- Salt and pepper, to taste
- Optional: red chili flakes for spice
- Fresh herbs for garnish (cilantro or parsley)

Instructions:

Preheat the oven to 400°F (200°C).
Pierce the eggplants with a fork and roast them in the oven until the skin is charred and the flesh is soft, about 30-40 minutes.
Remove the eggplants from the oven and let them cool slightly. Peel off the skin and mash the flesh with a fork or potato masher. Set aside.
In a pan, heat vegetable oil over medium heat. Sauté minced garlic until it becomes fragrant.
Add chopped tomatoes to the pan and cook until they break down and release their juices.
Stir in ground turmeric, salt, and pepper. Optionally, add red chili flakes for spice.
Add the mashed eggplant to the pan and mix well with the tomatoes and garlic.
Make wells in the eggplant mixture and crack the eggs into the wells. Scramble the eggs gently within the eggplant mixture until they are cooked through.
Continue to cook the Mirza Ghasemi for an additional 5-7 minutes, ensuring all ingredients are well combined and heated through.
Adjust the seasoning if needed and garnish with fresh herbs.
Serve Mirza Ghasemi warm with flatbread or as a side dish.

Enjoy this smoky and flavorful Persian eggplant and tomato dip! It's a delicious and comforting dish that can be enjoyed on its own or as part of a larger meal.

Lubia Polo (Green Bean Rice)

Ingredients:

- 2 cups Basmati rice
- 1 lb (about 450g) green beans, trimmed and cut into bite-sized pieces
- 1 large onion, finely chopped
- 500g ground beef or lamb
- 2 tablespoons tomato paste
- 1 teaspoon ground turmeric
- 1 teaspoon ground cumin
- Salt and pepper, to taste
- 3 tablespoons vegetable oil
- 1/2 cup raisins (optional)
- Saffron threads, dissolved in hot water (optional, for color and flavor)

Instructions:

Rinse the Basmati rice under cold water until the water runs clear. Soak the rice in water with some salt for about 2 hours.
In a large pot, bring water to a boil. Drain the soaked rice and add it to the boiling water. Cook until the rice is parboiled, about 6-8 minutes. Drain the rice.
In a pan, heat vegetable oil over medium heat. Sauté the chopped onions until golden brown.
Add ground beef or lamb to the pan and brown it. Drain any excess fat.
Stir in tomato paste, ground turmeric, ground cumin, salt, and pepper. Mix well and cook for a few minutes until the flavors meld.
Add the green beans to the meat mixture and sauté for 5-7 minutes until they are slightly tender.
In the same pot used for rice, layer the parboiled rice and the green bean and meat mixture. Repeat until all the rice and mixture are used.
Drizzle saffron water over the top layer of rice for color and flavor.
Optionally, add raisins between the layers for sweetness.
Create holes in the rice using the back of a wooden spoon handle to allow steam to escape.
Cover the pot with a clean kitchen towel and put the lid on top. Cook on low heat for about 45-50 minutes or until the rice is fully cooked and fluffy.
Once done, gently mix the rice and green beans together.
Serve Lubia Polo on a platter, and enjoy this flavorful Persian dish!

This rice dish is often served with a side of salad or yogurt. Enjoy your Lubia Polo!

Joojeh Kabab (Chicken Kebabs)

Ingredients:

- 2 pounds chicken thighs or breast, cut into chunks
- 1 cup plain yogurt
- 4 cloves garlic, minced
- Juice of 1 lemon
- 1 teaspoon ground saffron threads, dissolved in 2 tablespoons hot water
- 2 tablespoons olive oil
- 1 teaspoon ground turmeric
- Salt and pepper, to taste
- Skewers for grilling

Instructions:

In a bowl, mix together yogurt, minced garlic, lemon juice, saffron water, olive oil, ground turmeric, salt, and pepper to create the marinade.

Add chicken chunks to the marinade, ensuring they are well-coated. Marinate for at least 2 hours or overnight in the refrigerator.

Preheat the grill or oven to medium-high heat.

Thread marinated chicken pieces onto skewers.

Grill the chicken kebabs for about 15-20 minutes, turning occasionally, until they are cooked through and have a nice char.

Serve the Joojeh Kabab hot with rice or flatbread.

Enjoy these delicious Persian dishes!

Kalam Polo (Cabbage Rice)

Ingredients:

- 2 cups Basmati rice
- 1 medium-sized green cabbage, shredded
- 1 large onion, finely chopped
- 500g ground beef or lamb
- 2 tablespoons tomato paste
- 1 teaspoon ground turmeric
- Salt and pepper, to taste
- 1/4 cup vegetable oil
- 2 cups water
- 1/2 cup golden raisins (optional, for sweetness)
- 1/4 cup slivered almonds (for garnish)

Instructions:

Rinse the Basmati rice under cold water until the water runs clear. Soak the rice in water with some salt for about 2 hours.
In a pot, heat vegetable oil over medium heat. Sauté the chopped onions until they become golden brown.
Add ground meat to the pot and brown it on all sides.
Stir in tomato paste, ground turmeric, salt, and pepper. Mix well.
Add shredded cabbage to the pot and cook for a few minutes until it starts to soften.
Drain the soaked rice and add it to the pot, mixing it with the meat and cabbage.
Pour in water, cover the pot, and let it simmer on low heat for about 45-50 minutes or until the rice is fully cooked.
If using golden raisins, add them to the pot and mix them in for sweetness.
Once done, gently mix the rice, meat, cabbage, and raisins together.
In a separate pan, toast slivered almonds until they are golden brown.
Garnish Kalam Polo with toasted almonds before serving.

Enjoy this flavorful Persian Cabbage Rice! It can be served on its own or as a side dish with yogurt or a fresh salad.

Shirin Polo (Sweet Rice)

Ingredients:

- 2 cups Basmati rice
- 1/2 cup sugar (adjust to taste)
- 1/2 cup mixed dried fruits (apricots, raisins, barberries, dates, etc.)
- 1/2 cup mixed nuts (almonds, pistachios, slivered almonds, etc.)
- 1/4 cup vegetable oil or clarified butter (ghee)
- 1/2 teaspoon ground cinnamon
- 1/2 teaspoon ground cardamom
- 1/4 teaspoon ground saffron (dissolved in warm water)
- 1/4 teaspoon rose water (optional)
- Salt to taste
- Water for cooking rice

Instructions:

Prepare the Rice:
- Rinse the Basmati rice under cold water until the water runs clear. Soak the rice in water with a pinch of salt for at least 30 minutes.

Parboil the Rice:
- In a large pot, bring water to a boil. Drain the soaked rice and add it to the boiling water. Parboil the rice for about 5-7 minutes until it's slightly tender but still has a bite to it. Drain the rice.

Prepare the Sweet Mixture:
- In a separate bowl, mix sugar, dried fruits, nuts, ground cinnamon, ground cardamom, saffron water, and rose water if using.

Layer the Rice:
- In the same pot used for parboiling, layer the rice with the sweet mixture. Start with a layer of rice, followed by a layer of the sweet mixture. Repeat until both rice and sweet mixture are used up, with rice as the top layer.

Create Steam Holes:
- Use the handle of a wooden spoon to poke several holes through the rice to allow steam to escape.

Cook on Low Heat:
- Drizzle vegetable oil or clarified butter (ghee) over the top layer of rice. Cover the pot with a clean kitchen towel and a tight-fitting lid. Cook on low heat for about 45 minutes to 1 hour.

Fluff and Serve:

- Once the Shirin Polo is done, fluff the rice gently with a fork. Serve it on a platter, and you can garnish with additional nuts and dried fruits if desired.

Shirin Polo is often served as part of a festive meal and is enjoyed for its unique combination of sweetness and fragrant spices. It pairs well with a variety of Persian stews and kebabs.

Morasa Polo (Jeweled Rice)

Ingredients:

- 2 cups Basmati rice
- 1/2 cup sugar
- 1/2 cup mixed dried fruits (barberries, apricots, raisins, etc.)
- 1/2 cup mixed nuts (almonds, pistachios, slivered almonds, etc.)
- 1/4 cup orange peel, finely chopped
- 1/4 cup butter or vegetable oil
- 1/2 teaspoon ground saffron (dissolved in warm water)
- 1/4 teaspoon ground cinnamon
- 1/4 teaspoon ground cardamom
- Salt to taste
- Water for cooking rice

Instructions:

Prepare the Rice:
- Rinse the Basmati rice under cold water until the water runs clear. Soak the rice in water with a pinch of salt for at least 30 minutes.

Parboil the Rice:
- In a large pot, bring water to a boil. Drain the soaked rice and add it to the boiling water. Parboil the rice for about 5-7 minutes until it's slightly tender but still has a bite to it. Drain the rice.

Prepare the Sweet Mixture:
- In a separate bowl, mix sugar, dried fruits, nuts, orange peel, ground saffron, ground cinnamon, and ground cardamom.

Layer the Rice:
- In the same pot used for parboiling, layer the rice with the sweet mixture. Start with a layer of rice, followed by a layer of the sweet mixture. Repeat until both rice and sweet mixture are used up, with rice as the top layer.

Create Steam Holes:
- Use the handle of a wooden spoon to poke several holes through the rice to allow steam to escape.

Cook on Low Heat:
- Drizzle butter or vegetable oil over the top layer of rice. Cover the pot with a clean kitchen towel and a tight-fitting lid. Cook on low heat for about 45 minutes to 1 hour.

Fluff and Serve:
- Once the Morasa Polo is done, fluff the rice gently with a fork. Serve it on a platter, and you can garnish with additional nuts and dried fruits for an extra touch of elegance.

Morasa Polo is a visually stunning dish that adds a festive touch to special occasions. It's often served as a centerpiece at celebrations and pairs well with a variety of Persian dishes.

Mast-o Khiar (Cucumber Yogurt)

Ingredients:

- 2 cups Greek yogurt (or strained plain yogurt)
- 1 cucumber, peeled and finely grated
- 2 cloves garlic, minced
- 1 tablespoon dried mint (or 2 tablespoons fresh mint, chopped)
- 1 tablespoon fresh dill, chopped
- 1 tablespoon fresh chives or green onions, finely chopped
- 1 tablespoon extra virgin olive oil
- Salt and pepper to taste

Instructions:

Prepare the Cucumber:
- Peel the cucumber and grate it finely. If the cucumber has a lot of water, you can squeeze out some of the excess moisture.

Mix Yogurt and Cucumber:
- In a mixing bowl, combine Greek yogurt and grated cucumber. Mix well.

Add Garlic and Herbs:
- Add minced garlic, dried mint (or fresh mint), chopped fresh dill, and chopped chives (or green onions) to the yogurt-cucumber mixture.

Season and Drizzle with Olive Oil:
- Season the Mast-o Khiar with salt and pepper to taste. Drizzle extra virgin olive oil over the top.

Mix Well:
- Mix all the ingredients well, ensuring that the yogurt and cucumber are evenly combined with the herbs and garlic.

Chill:
- Cover the bowl and refrigerate the Mast-o Khiar for at least 1-2 hours to allow the flavors to meld and the dish to chill.

Serve:
- Before serving, give the Mast-o Khiar a final stir. Serve it chilled as a refreshing side dish.

Mast-o Khiar is a versatile accompaniment that pairs well with a variety of Persian dishes. It can be served alongside rice dishes, kebabs, or as a dip with flatbread. Enjoy its cooling and tangy flavors, especially during warmer weather or as part of a festive spread.

Loobia Polo (Persian Rice with Green Beans)

Ingredients:

- 2 cups Basmati rice
- 1/2 pound (about 225g) green beans, ends trimmed and cut into small pieces
- 1 pound (about 500g) ground beef or lamb
- 1 large onion, finely chopped
- 2 cloves garlic, minced
- 1 teaspoon ground turmeric
- 1 teaspoon ground cumin
- 1 teaspoon ground cinnamon
- Salt and pepper to taste
- 1/2 cup tomato sauce or 2 tablespoons tomato paste
- 1/4 cup vegetable oil
- 1/4 cup slivered almonds or chopped pistachios (optional, for garnish)
- Saffron threads, dissolved in warm water (for coloring and flavor)

Instructions:

Prepare the Rice:
- Rinse the Basmati rice under cold water until the water runs clear. Soak the rice in water with a pinch of salt for at least 30 minutes.

Blanch the Green Beans:
- Bring a pot of water to boil and blanch the green beans for 2-3 minutes until they are slightly tender. Drain and set aside.

Sauté Onion and Garlic:
- In a large pan, heat vegetable oil over medium heat. Sauté chopped onions until golden brown. Add minced garlic and sauté for an additional minute.

Cook Ground Meat:
- Add ground meat to the pan and cook until browned. Break the meat into small pieces using a spatula.

Add Spices and Tomato Sauce:
- Stir in ground turmeric, ground cumin, ground cinnamon, salt, and pepper. Add tomato sauce (or tomato paste) and mix well. Cook for a few minutes until the flavors meld.

Combine with Green Beans:
- Add the blanched green beans to the meat mixture and cook for an additional 5 minutes. Adjust seasoning if needed.

Prepare Rice Layers:
- In a separate pot, parboil the soaked rice for about 5-7 minutes until it's slightly tender. Drain the rice.
- In the same pot, layer the parboiled rice with the meat and green bean mixture. Repeat until both rice and meat-green bean mixture are used up, with rice as the top layer.

Create Steam Holes:
- Use the handle of a wooden spoon to poke several holes through the rice to allow steam to escape.

Cook on Low Heat:
- Drizzle saffron-infused water over the top layer of rice. Cover the pot with a clean kitchen towel and a tight-fitting lid. Cook on low heat for about 45 minutes to 1 hour.

Garnish:
- Before serving, fluff the rice gently with a fork and garnish with slivered almonds or chopped pistachios if desired.

Serve:
- Serve Loobia Polo on a platter, allowing the colorful layers to be displayed. Enjoy!

Loobia Polo is a delicious and aromatic dish that combines the richness of ground meat with the freshness of green beans. It's often served with a side of Mast-o Khiar (cucumber yogurt) or a simple salad.

Zeytoon Parvardeh (Marinated Olives)

Ingredients:

- 2 cups green or black olives, pitted
- 2 tablespoons pomegranate molasses
- 2 tablespoons walnut paste or finely ground walnuts
- 2 cloves garlic, minced
- 1 tablespoon fresh mint, chopped
- 1 tablespoon fresh cilantro, chopped
- 1 tablespoon fresh parsley, chopped
- 1 teaspoon ground coriander
- 1 teaspoon ground cumin
- 1/2 teaspoon red pepper flakes (adjust to taste)
- 1/4 cup extra virgin olive oil
- Salt and pepper to taste

Instructions:

Prepare the Olives:
- If the olives are not pitted, pit them. You can use green or black olives based on your preference.

Make the Marinade:
- In a bowl, combine pomegranate molasses, walnut paste or ground walnuts, minced garlic, chopped fresh mint, cilantro, and parsley.

Add Spices:
- Stir in ground coriander, ground cumin, red pepper flakes, salt, and pepper.

Combine with Olives:
- Add the pitted olives to the marinade and toss them well to ensure they are coated evenly.

Drizzle with Olive Oil:
- Drizzle extra virgin olive oil over the olives and mix again.

Marinate:
- Allow the olives to marinate in the refrigerator for at least 2-3 hours, or preferably overnight. This allows the flavors to meld.

Serve:
- Before serving, bring the marinated olives to room temperature. Transfer them to a serving dish and garnish with additional herbs if desired.

Enjoy:

- Zeytoon Parvardeh is ready to be enjoyed as a flavorful and tangy appetizer or side dish.

Zeytoon Parvardeh is known for its bold and zesty flavors, making it a perfect accompaniment for gatherings or as part of a mezze platter. The combination of pomegranate molasses, walnuts, and aromatic herbs adds a unique and delightful taste to the olives.

Asheh Reshteh (Noodle and Herb Soup)

Ingredients:

- 1 cup lentils, rinsed
- 1 cup chickpeas, soaked overnight (or canned)
- 1 cup kidney beans, soaked overnight (or canned)
- 1 cup chopped leeks or onions
- 4 cups chopped mixed fresh herbs (parsley, cilantro, dill, green onions)
- 1 cup spinach, chopped
- 1 cup Persian noodles (Reshteh) or linguine, broken into small pieces
- 1/2 cup chopped mint (optional, for garnish)
- 1/4 cup vegetable oil
- 1 large onion, finely chopped
- 3 cloves garlic, minced
- 1 teaspoon turmeric
- Salt and pepper to taste
- 8 cups water or vegetable broth
- 1 cup kashk (Persian whey, available in Middle Eastern stores) or Greek yogurt (as a substitute)

Instructions:

Prepare Legumes:
- In a large pot, combine lentils, chickpeas, kidney beans, and chopped leeks or onions. Add water or vegetable broth. Bring to a boil and then simmer until the legumes are tender.

Add Herbs:
- Add chopped fresh herbs and spinach to the pot. Simmer for an additional 10-15 minutes.

Sauté Onion and Garlic:
- In a separate pan, heat vegetable oil over medium heat. Sauté finely chopped onions until golden brown. Add minced garlic and sauté for an additional minute.

Add Turmeric:
- Stir in turmeric and continue sautéing for another minute to release the fragrance.

Combine with Soup:
- Add the sautéed onion and garlic mixture to the pot of legumes and herbs. Mix well and let it simmer.

Cook Noodles:
- Cook the Persian noodles (Reshteh) or linguine according to the package instructions. Drain and add the noodles to the soup.

Season:
- Season the soup with salt and pepper to taste. Adjust the seasoning as needed.

Serve:
- Ladle the soup into bowls. Garnish with chopped mint and a dollop of kashk or Greek yogurt.

Enjoy:
- Asheh Reshteh is ready to be enjoyed. Serve it hot with additional herbs and a squeeze of lemon if desired.

Asheh Reshteh is a comforting and nutritious soup that's often enjoyed during special occasions and celebrations in Persian cuisine. It brings together a delightful mix of legumes, herbs, and noodles.

Koofteh Berenji (Rice Meatballs)

Ingredients:

For the Meatballs:

- 1 cup short-grain rice
- 1 pound ground beef or lamb
- 1 large onion, grated
- 1 cup mixed fresh herbs (parsley, cilantro, dill), finely chopped
- 1/2 cup yellow split peas, soaked
- 2 tablespoons advieh (Persian spice mix) or a combination of ground cumin, cinnamon, and nutmeg
- Salt and pepper to taste

For the Filling:

- 1/2 cup ground walnuts
- 1/4 cup dried barberries (zereshk), soaked in water
- 1 teaspoon ground cinnamon
- 1 teaspoon sugar
- Salt to taste

For the Sauce:

- 1 large onion, thinly sliced
- 2 tablespoons tomato paste
- 1/4 cup vegetable oil
- 1 teaspoon advieh (Persian spice mix) or a combination of ground cumin, cinnamon, and nutmeg
- 2 cups water
- Salt and pepper to taste

Instructions:

Prepare the Meatball Mixture:
- Rinse the short-grain rice and cook it until it's slightly tender. Drain and let it cool.
- In a large mixing bowl, combine the cooked rice, ground meat, grated onion, chopped herbs, soaked yellow split peas, advieh (spice mix), salt, and pepper. Mix well.

Prepare the Filling:

- In a separate bowl, mix ground walnuts, drained barberries, ground cinnamon, sugar, and salt. This will be the filling for the meatballs.

Form the Meatballs:
  - Take a portion of the meatball mixture in your hand, make an indentation in the center, and add a small amount of the walnut-barberry filling. Close the meatball around the filling, shaping it into a large round ball. Repeat for the remaining mixture.

Prepare the Sauce:
  - In a pot, sauté thinly sliced onions in vegetable oil until golden brown. Add tomato paste and sauté for an additional 2-3 minutes.
  - Add advieh (spice mix), water, salt, and pepper. Bring the sauce to a simmer.

Cook the Meatballs:
  - Gently place the shaped meatballs into the simmering sauce. Cover the pot and let it cook on low heat for about 1.5 to 2 hours until the meatballs are cooked through.

Serve:
  - Carefully transfer the Koofteh Berenji to a serving platter. Spoon some of the sauce over the top.

Enjoy:
  - Koofteh Berenji is ready to be enjoyed. Serve it with rice, flatbread, or on its own.

Koofteh Berenji is a flavorful and comforting dish with a delicious surprise of filling inside each meatball. It's often served on special occasions and gatherings in Persian cuisine.

Shirazi Salad (Cucumber Tomato Salad)

Ingredients:

- 2 medium-sized cucumbers, diced
- 4 medium-sized tomatoes, diced
- 1 small red onion, finely chopped
- 1/4 cup fresh mint, chopped
- 1/4 cup fresh parsley, chopped
- Juice of 1-2 lemons
- 2 tablespoons extra virgin olive oil
- Salt and pepper to taste

Instructions:

Prepare the Vegetables:
- Wash and dice the cucumbers and tomatoes into small, bite-sized pieces.

Chop Herbs and Onion:
- Finely chop fresh mint, parsley, and the red onion.

Combine Ingredients:
- In a large bowl, combine the diced cucumbers, tomatoes, chopped mint, chopped parsley, and finely chopped red onion.

Dress the Salad:
- Drizzle the salad with fresh lemon juice and extra virgin olive oil. Toss the salad gently to coat the ingredients with the dressing.

Season:
- Season the Shirazi Salad with salt and pepper according to your taste. Toss again to ensure even seasoning.

Chill (Optional):
- You can refrigerate the salad for about 30 minutes if you prefer it chilled before serving.

Serve:
- Transfer the Shirazi Salad to a serving dish or individual plates.

Enjoy:
- Shirazi Salad is ready to be enjoyed as a refreshing side dish alongside Persian main courses or as a standalone salad.

This simple and vibrant salad is a staple in Persian cuisine, adding a burst of freshness to meals. It's particularly popular during the warm months and complements various dishes with its crisp texture and tangy flavors.

Baghali Polo Ba Mahicheh (Dill and Lima Bean Rice with Lamb)

Ingredients:

For the Rice:

- 2 cups Basmati rice
- 1/2 cup vegetable oil
- Salt

For the Baghali (Lima Beans):

- 2 cups frozen or fresh lima beans
- 2 tablespoons butter
- Salt

For the Mahicheh (Lamb):

- 1 pound lamb shoulder or leg, cubed
- 1 large onion, finely chopped
- 2 tablespoons vegetable oil
- 1 teaspoon turmeric
- Salt and pepper to taste

For the Dill Mixture:

- 2 cups fresh dill, chopped
- 2 cloves garlic, minced
- 2 tablespoons vegetable oil

Instructions:

Prepare the Rice:
- Rinse the Basmati rice under cold water until the water runs clear. Soak the rice in water with a pinch of salt for at least 30 minutes.
- In a large pot, bring water to a boil. Add the soaked and drained rice. Cook until the rice is parboiled (partially cooked) but still has a bite to it. Drain the rice.
- In the same pot, heat vegetable oil. Add a layer of parboiled rice, followed by a layer of dill mixture, and then continue layering until both are used up. Finish with a layer of rice.

Prepare the Baghali (Lima Beans):

- Cook the lima beans in boiling water with salt until they are tender. Drain and set aside.
- In a pan, melt butter and sauté the cooked lima beans for a few minutes. Set aside.

Prepare the Mahicheh (Lamb):
- In a separate pan, heat vegetable oil over medium heat. Sauté finely chopped onions until golden brown.
- Add cubed lamb to the pan and brown on all sides. Season with turmeric, salt, and pepper.
- Add water to the pan, cover, and simmer until the lamb is cooked and tender.

Combine Ingredients:
- Gently mix the cooked lima beans with the lamb and its juices.
- Create a well in the center of the layered rice and pour the lamb and lima bean mixture into the well.
- Cover the pot with a clean kitchen towel and a tight-fitting lid. Cook on low heat for about 45 minutes to 1 hour.

Serve:
- Before serving, gently fluff the rice with a fork, allowing the dill and lima beans to distribute evenly.
- Serve Baghali Polo Ba Mahicheh on a platter, presenting the layers of rice, dill, lima beans, and lamb.

Enjoy:
- Baghali Polo Ba Mahicheh is ready to be enjoyed. Serve it with a side of yogurt or a fresh salad.

This dish is a delightful combination of flavors and textures, and it's often enjoyed on special occasions and celebrations in Persian cuisine.

Abgoosht (Persian Meat Soup)

Ingredients:

For the Soup Base:

- 1 pound lamb or beef shanks
- 1 pound lamb or beef neck bones
- 1 large onion, peeled and halved
- 2 tomatoes, halved
- 1 large potato, peeled and halved
- 1 large carrot, peeled and halved
- 1 teaspoon turmeric
- Salt and pepper to taste
- Water

For the Separated Ingredients:

- 1 cup chickpeas, soaked overnight
- 1 cup white beans, soaked overnight
- 1 cup dried yellow split peas
- 4 medium-sized potatoes, peeled and quartered
- 4 tomatoes, quartered
- 4 green bell peppers, halved and seeded
- 4 cloves garlic, peeled
- 1 tablespoon dried mint (optional, for garnish)

For Serving:

- Sangak or Lavash bread
- Radishes
- Fresh herbs (mint, tarragon, basil)

Instructions:

Prepare the Soup Base:
- In a large pot, combine lamb or beef shanks, neck bones, halved onion, halved tomatoes, halved potato, halved carrot, turmeric, salt, and pepper.
- Cover the ingredients with water. Bring to a boil and then reduce the heat to simmer. Skim off any foam that rises to the surface.

- Simmer for about 2 to 3 hours until the meat is tender and the broth is flavorful.

Separate and Mash:
- Once the meat is cooked, remove it from the broth and set it aside. Strain the broth to remove solids, leaving a clear broth.
- Mash the cooked vegetables from the broth (onion, tomato, potato, carrot) and add them back to the clear broth.

Cook Separated Ingredients:
- In separate pots, cook chickpeas, white beans, and yellow split peas until they are tender.
- In another pot, cook quartered potatoes, quartered tomatoes, halved green bell peppers, and peeled garlic cloves.

Serve:
- Serve the clear broth with mashed vegetables alongside the separated ingredients (meat, chickpeas, white beans, yellow split peas, potatoes, tomatoes, bell peppers, garlic).
- Garnish with dried mint if desired.

Enjoy:
- Abgoosht is traditionally eaten with Sangak or Lavash bread. Tear off a piece of bread, dip it in the broth, and enjoy it with the meats and vegetables.

Serving Suggestions:
- Serve with radishes and fresh herbs on the side for added freshness.

Abgoosht is a communal dish, often enjoyed with family and friends. The broth is sipped separately, and the meats and vegetables are typically mashed and eaten with bread. It's a comforting and hearty dish, perfect for gatherings.

Kufteh Tabrizi (Tabriz-style Meatballs)

Ingredients:

For the Meatballs:

- 1 pound ground beef or lamb
- 1 cup rice, soaked in warm water for a couple of hours
- 1 large onion, grated
- 1/2 cup yellow split peas, soaked in water for a few hours
- 1/2 cup dried chickpeas, soaked in water for a few hours
- 1/4 cup dried lentils, soaked in water for a few hours
- 1/4 cup dried dill, finely chopped
- 1/4 cup dried tarragon, finely chopped
- 1/4 cup dried mint, finely chopped
- 1/4 cup fresh parsley, chopped
- 1/4 cup chopped walnuts
- 1/4 cup barberries (zereshk), soaked in water
- 2 eggs
- 1 teaspoon ground cinnamon
- 1 teaspoon ground turmeric
- Salt and pepper to taste
- Oil for frying

For the Filling:

- 100 grams prunes
- 100 grams walnut halves

For the Sauce:

- 2 large onions, thinly sliced
- 1 tablespoon tomato paste
- 1/2 cup vegetable oil
- 1 teaspoon ground turmeric
- Salt and pepper to taste
- 2 cups water

Instructions:

Prepare the Filling:

- Pit the prunes and stuff them with walnut halves. Set aside.

Prepare the Meatball Mixture:
- Drain the soaked rice, yellow split peas, chickpeas, and lentils. In a food processor, combine the ground meat, grated onion, soaked and drained rice, split peas, chickpeas, and lentils.
- Add eggs, dried dill, dried tarragon, dried mint, fresh parsley, chopped walnuts, barberries, ground cinnamon, ground turmeric, salt, and pepper. Process until you get a well-combined mixture.

Assemble the Meatballs:
- Take a handful of the meat mixture, flatten it in your palm, place a stuffed prune-walnut in the center, and shape the meat around it to form a large meatball.

Fry the Meatballs:
- Heat oil in a deep pan. Fry the meatballs until they are golden brown on all sides. Be gentle when turning them to avoid breaking.

Prepare the Sauce:
- In a separate pot, sauté thinly sliced onions in vegetable oil until golden brown. Add tomato paste, ground turmeric, salt, and pepper. Mix well.
- Pour in water and bring the sauce to a simmer.

Simmer the Meatballs:
- Transfer the fried meatballs into the simmering sauce. Cover the pot and let it cook on low heat for about 1.5 to 2 hours until the meatballs are fully cooked and the flavors meld.

Serve:
- Serve Kufteh Tabrizi hot, with some of the sauce poured over the top.

Enjoy:
- Kufteh Tabrizi is traditionally served with Persian rice. Enjoy this flavorful and unique dish!

Kufteh Tabrizi is known for its rich and diverse flavors, making it a special and beloved dish in Iranian cuisine. The combination of meat, rice, and a delightful filling creates a memorable dining experience.

Maast-o Esfenaj (Yogurt and Spinach Dip)

Ingredients:

- 2 cups Greek yogurt
- 1 cup fresh spinach, finely chopped
- 2 tablespoons dried mint
- 2 cloves garlic, minced
- 1 tablespoon olive oil
- 1 tablespoon lime or lemon juice
- Salt and pepper to taste
- Walnuts for garnish (optional)

Instructions:

Prepare the Yogurt Base:
- In a mixing bowl, combine Greek yogurt, minced garlic, and olive oil.

Add Spinach:
- Finely chop fresh spinach and add it to the yogurt mixture.

Seasoning:
- Add dried mint, lime or lemon juice, salt, and pepper to the bowl.

Mix Well:
- Mix all the ingredients well until they are thoroughly combined.

Chill (Optional):
- For enhanced flavors, you can refrigerate the Maast-o Esfenaj for at least 1-2 hours before serving.

Garnish:
- Optionally, garnish the dip with chopped walnuts for added texture and flavor.

Serve:
- Transfer the Maast-o Esfenaj to a serving bowl.

Enjoy:
- Serve the yogurt and spinach dip with pita bread, naan, or as a side dish to complement your meal.

Maast-o Esfenaj is a delicious and cooling dip that pairs well with a variety of dishes. It's a common feature in Persian cuisine, offering a delightful combination of creamy yogurt, vibrant spinach, and aromatic herbs.

Dizi (Persian Lamb Stew)

Ingredients:

For the Stew:

- 1.5 pounds lamb shoulder, cut into chunks
- 1 cup chickpeas, soaked overnight
- 1 cup white beans, soaked overnight
- 1 large onion, chopped
- 3-4 cloves garlic, minced
- 2 large tomatoes, chopped
- 2 large potatoes, peeled and cut into chunks
- 2 large carrots, peeled and cut into chunks
- 1 cup celery, chopped
- 1 teaspoon turmeric
- Salt and pepper to taste
- Water

For the Side Dishes:

- Sangak or Lavash bread
- Fresh herbs (mint, tarragon, basil)
- Radishes
- Salt
- Lime or lemon wedges

Instructions:

Prepare the Stew:
- In a large pot, combine lamb chunks, soaked chickpeas, soaked white beans, chopped onion, minced garlic, chopped tomatoes, turmeric, salt, and pepper.
- Add enough water to cover the ingredients. Bring to a boil and then reduce the heat to simmer. Skim off any foam that rises to the surface.
- Simmer for about 2-3 hours until the lamb is tender and the beans are cooked.

Separate Solids and Broth:
- Once the stew is cooked, separate the solids (lamb, beans, vegetables) from the broth. Set aside the broth.

Mash the Solids:

- Place the solids in a large bowl and mash them with a potato masher or fork until they form a coarse paste. This is known as "Ghooreh."

Serve:
- Heat the broth to serve as a soup on the side.
- Serve the mashed solids (Ghooreh) on a plate or in a bowl. Accompany with Sangak or Lavash bread.

Serving Tradition:
- Dizi is traditionally eaten by tearing off a piece of bread, dipping it in the broth, and then taking a bite of the mashed solids. Radishes and fresh herbs can be enjoyed on the side.

Enhance with Lime or Lemon:
- Squeeze lime or lemon over the mashed solids for an extra burst of flavor.

Enjoy:
- Dizi is a communal and hearty meal enjoyed with family and friends. It's a unique and flavorful experience in Persian cuisine.

Dizi is not only a delicious stew but also a cultural and social tradition in Persian dining. The combination of flavors and the interactive serving method make it a memorable and enjoyable dish.

Sheer Khurma (Milk and Date Pudding)
Ingredients:

- 1 cup vermicelli, broken into small pieces
- 1/4 cup ghee (clarified butter)
- 1-liter whole milk
- 1 cup sugar (adjust to taste)
- 1/2 cup dates, chopped
- 1/4 cup almonds, sliced
- 1/4 cup pistachios, sliced
- 1/4 cup cashews, chopped
- 1/4 cup raisins
- 1/2 teaspoon cardamom powder
- A pinch of saffron strands (optional)
- Rose water or kewra water (optional, for fragrance)

Instructions:

Prepare Vermicelli:
- In a pan, heat ghee over medium heat. Add broken vermicelli and sauté until it turns golden brown. Keep stirring to prevent burning.

Boil Milk:
- In a separate pot, bring whole milk to a boil. Once it boils, reduce the heat to low and let it simmer.

Add Vermicelli:
- Add the roasted vermicelli to the simmering milk. Cook until the vermicelli becomes soft, stirring occasionally.

Sweeten the Pudding:
- Add sugar to the milk and vermicelli. Stir well until the sugar dissolves. Adjust the sweetness according to your taste.

Add Dates and Nuts:
- Add chopped dates, sliced almonds, sliced pistachios, chopped cashews, and raisins to the pudding. Mix well.

Flavor with Cardamom:
- Add cardamom powder to the pudding for aromatic flavor. If using saffron strands, dissolve them in a little warm milk and add to the pudding.

Simmer:

- Let the Sheer Khurma simmer on low heat for about 10-15 minutes until it reaches the desired consistency. The pudding should be thick and creamy.

Add Fragrance (Optional):
- If desired, add a few drops of rose water or kewra water to enhance the fragrance of the dessert.

Serve Warm or Chilled:
- Sheer Khurma can be served warm or chilled. It thickens as it cools, so adjust the consistency accordingly.

Garnish and Serve:
- Garnish with additional nuts and raisins. Serve Sheer Khurma in bowls or dessert dishes.

Enjoy:
- Sheer Khurma is ready to be enjoyed. It's a delightful and festive dessert that is often shared with family and friends.

Sheer Khurma is not only a delicious dessert but also a symbol of celebration and togetherness during special occasions. The combination of creamy milk, sweet dates, and assorted nuts makes it a cherished treat.

Faloodeh Shirazi (Rosewater Sorbet)
Ingredients:

- 1 cup rice starch vermicelli or cornstarch noodles
- 4 cups water
- 1 cup sugar (adjust to taste)
- 1/4 cup rose water
- Juice of 2-3 lemons
- Crushed ice for serving
- Optional garnishes: chopped pistachios or slivered almonds

Instructions:

    Prepare the Noodles:
- Cook the rice starch vermicelli or cornstarch noodles according to the package instructions. Drain and set aside.

    Make Simple Syrup:
- In a saucepan, combine water and sugar. Bring to a boil, stirring to dissolve the sugar. Allow the syrup to cool.

    Combine Ingredients:
- In a mixing bowl, combine the cooked noodles, rose water, and lemon juice.

    Mix with Simple Syrup:
- Gradually add the cooled simple syrup to the noodle mixture. Stir well to combine. Adjust the sweetness by adding more sugar if needed.

    Chill:
- Place the mixture in the refrigerator to chill for at least 2 hours.

    Freeze:
- Pour the chilled mixture into a shallow dish and place it in the freezer.
- Every 30 minutes, use a fork to stir the mixture, breaking up any ice crystals. Repeat this process until the mixture is completely frozen and has a slushy texture.

    Serve:
- When ready to serve, fluff the Faloodeh with a fork to create a snow-like texture.

    Garnish (Optional):
- Garnish with chopped pistachios or slivered almonds if desired.

    Serve with Crushed Ice:

- Serve Faloodeh Shirazi in bowls or glasses over crushed ice.

Enjoy:
- Faloodeh Shirazi is ready to be enjoyed as a cool and refreshing dessert, especially on a hot day.

Faloodeh Shirazi is a delightful and unique dessert that combines the cooling properties of rose water and lemon with the fun texture of frozen noodles. It's a popular choice during the warm months in Persian cuisine.

Khoresh-e Karafs (Celery Stew)

Ingredients:

- 1 pound (about 500g) lamb or beef, cut into cubes
- 4 cups celery, chopped into 1-inch pieces
- 1 large onion, finely chopped
- 3 tablespoons vegetable oil
- 2 teaspoons turmeric
- 1 teaspoon cinnamon
- Salt and pepper to taste
- 2 cups chopped parsley
- 1 cup chopped mint
- 2 tablespoons dried fenugreek leaves (optional)
- 1 tablespoon tomato paste
- 1-2 lemons, juiced
- 2 cups water or beef broth
- 1 tablespoon flour (optional, for thickening)
- Steamed rice for serving

Instructions:

Sauté Onions:
- In a large pot, heat vegetable oil over medium heat. Sauté finely chopped onions until golden brown.

Brown the Meat:
- Add the cubed meat to the pot and brown on all sides.

Add Spices:
- Stir in turmeric, cinnamon, salt, and pepper. Mix well to coat the meat with the spices.

Add Tomato Paste:
- Add tomato paste to the pot and continue stirring for a couple of minutes.

Add Vegetables:
- Add chopped celery to the pot and mix with the meat and spices.

Pour Water or Broth:
- Pour water or beef broth into the pot, ensuring that the ingredients are fully covered.

Simmer:

- Bring the stew to a boil, then reduce the heat to low, cover the pot, and let it simmer for about 1.5 to 2 hours or until the meat is tender and the flavors meld.

Add Herbs:
- About 30 minutes before serving, add chopped parsley, chopped mint, and dried fenugreek leaves (if using) to the pot. Mix well.

Adjust Seasoning:
- Taste the stew and adjust the seasoning if needed. If you prefer a hint of acidity, you can add lemon juice.

Optional Thickening:
- If you prefer a thicker stew, you can mix a tablespoon of flour with a little water to create a smooth paste. Add it to the stew and simmer for an additional 10-15 minutes.

Serve:
- Serve the Khoresh-e Karafs over steamed rice.

Enjoy:
- Khoresh-e Karafs is ready to be enjoyed. It's a savory and aromatic stew with the unique flavor of celery.

Khoresh-e Karafs is a comforting and nourishing dish that showcases the rich flavors of Persian cuisine. The combination of meat, celery, and herbs creates a hearty and delicious stew.

Morgh Polo (Chicken Rice)

Ingredients:

For the Chicken:

- 1 whole chicken, cut into pieces
- 2 onions, finely chopped
- 2 tablespoons vegetable oil
- 1 teaspoon turmeric
- Salt and pepper to taste
- 1 cup water

For the Rice:

- 2 cups Basmati rice
- 4 cups water
- Salt to taste

For the Garnish:

- 1/2 cup barberries, washed and soaked in water
- 2 tablespoons sugar
- 2 tablespoons butter or oil
- Saffron threads, soaked in warm water

Optional Additions:

- Sliced almonds or pistachios for garnish

Instructions:

Prepare the Chicken:
- In a pot, heat vegetable oil over medium heat. Sauté finely chopped onions until golden brown.
- Add turmeric, salt, and pepper. Stir well.
- Add chicken pieces to the pot and brown them on all sides.
- Pour in water, cover the pot, and let the chicken cook until tender.

Cook the Rice:
- Rinse Basmati rice under cold water until the water runs clear.
- In a separate pot, bring 4 cups of water to a boil. Add salt and rice to the boiling water.

- Cook the rice until it's parboiled (partially cooked) and still has a bite to it. Drain the rice.

Layering:
- In the pot with the cooked chicken, make a layer of parboiled rice over the chicken.
- Repeat the layers until both chicken and rice are used up. Finish with a layer of rice on top.

Create Steam:
- Using the handle of a wooden spoon, poke a few holes in the rice to allow steam to escape.
- Pour saffron-infused water over the top layer of rice.
- Cover the pot with a clean kitchen towel and a tight-fitting lid. Cook on low heat for about 1 to 1.5 hours.

Prepare Barberry Garnish:
- In a small pan, heat butter or oil. Add soaked barberries and sugar. Sauté for a few minutes until the barberries are plump.

Garnish and Serve:
- Once the Morgh Polo is ready, fluff the rice gently with a fork.
- Serve the chicken rice on a platter, and garnish with the sautéed barberries and sliced almonds or pistachios if desired.

Enjoy:
- Morgh Polo is ready to be enjoyed. Serve it with a side of yogurt.

Morgh Polo is a delicious and fragrant dish that highlights the aromatic flavors of Persian cuisine. The combination of tender chicken, seasoned rice, and the sweet-tart barberry garnish creates a delightful meal.

Mast-o Khiar Ba Mosamma (Cucumber Yogurt with Mint)
Ingredients:

- 2 cups Greek yogurt
- 1 cucumber, grated
- 2 tablespoons fresh mint, finely chopped
- 1 clove garlic, minced
- 1 tablespoon dried mint
- Salt to taste
- 1 tablespoon extra-virgin olive oil (optional)
- Walnuts for garnish (optional)

Instructions:

Prepare the Yogurt:
- In a mixing bowl, combine Greek yogurt with minced garlic.

Grate Cucumber:
- Peel and grate the cucumber. Squeeze out any excess water from the grated cucumber.

Add Cucumber and Fresh Mint:
- Add the grated cucumber and finely chopped fresh mint to the yogurt. Mix well.

Seasoning:
- Add dried mint and salt to the mixture. Adjust the seasoning according to your taste.

Optional Olive Oil:
- Drizzle extra-virgin olive oil over the top for added richness and flavor. This step is optional.

Chill:
- Refrigerate the Mast-o Khiar for at least 1-2 hours before serving to allow the flavors to meld.

Garnish (Optional):
- Garnish with chopped walnuts if desired.

Serve:
- Mast-o Khiar Ba Mosamma is ready to be served. It can be enjoyed as a side dish, dip, or accompaniment to main courses.

Enjoy:

- Serve chilled and enjoy the cool and refreshing taste of Mast-o Khiar Ba Mosamma.

This yogurt dish is known for its cooling properties and is a perfect complement to spicy or flavorful dishes. It's a versatile side that adds a burst of freshness to your meal.

Gondi (Chickpea and Chicken Dumplings)

Ingredients:

For the Dumplings:

- 1 cup chickpea flour (besan)
- 1 cup ground chicken
- 1 large onion, grated
- 1 cup finely chopped fresh herbs (parsley, cilantro, dill)
- 1 teaspoon ground turmeric
- 1 teaspoon ground cumin
- 1 teaspoon baking soda
- Salt and pepper to taste
- 1/2 cup vegetable oil (for frying)

For the Soup:

- 8 cups chicken broth
- 1 large onion, chopped
- 2 carrots, sliced
- 2 celery stalks, sliced
- 2 cloves garlic, minced
- 1 teaspoon ground turmeric
- Salt and pepper to taste
- Fresh herbs for garnish (parsley, cilantro)

Instructions:

   Prepare the Dumplings:
   - In a large mixing bowl, combine chickpea flour, ground chicken, grated onion, chopped herbs, ground turmeric, ground cumin, baking soda, salt, and pepper.
   - Mix the ingredients well to form a thick batter. If needed, add a little water to achieve the right consistency.

   Shape the Dumplings:
   - With wet hands, shape the batter into small, round dumplings.

   Fry the Dumplings:
   - Heat vegetable oil in a pan over medium heat. Fry the dumplings until they are golden brown on all sides. Remove and set aside.

   Prepare the Soup:

- In a large pot, sauté chopped onion and minced garlic until golden brown.
- Add ground turmeric and continue to sauté for a minute.
- Pour in chicken broth and bring it to a simmer.
- Add sliced carrots and celery to the pot. Cook until the vegetables are tender.

Add Dumplings to the Soup:

- Gently place the fried dumplings into the simmering soup.

Season:

- Season the soup with salt and pepper according to your taste. Simmer for an additional 10-15 minutes.

Garnish and Serve:

- Garnish the Gondi soup with fresh herbs such as parsley or cilantro.

Enjoy:

- Serve the Gondi hot, and enjoy the flavorful combination of chickpea and chicken in a comforting soup.

Gondi is a unique and flavorful dish that brings together the richness of chickpea and chicken in dumpling form, creating a delightful and hearty meal.

Baghali Polo Ba Morgh (Dill and Lima Bean Rice with Chicken)
Ingredients:

For the Chicken:

- 1 whole chicken, cut into pieces
- 2 onions, finely chopped
- 3 tablespoons vegetable oil
- 1 teaspoon turmeric
- Salt and pepper to taste
- 1 cup water

For the Rice:

- 2 cups Basmati rice
- 4 cups water
- Salt to taste

For the Baghali Polo (Dill and Lima Bean Rice):

- 2 cups frozen lima beans
- 1 cup fresh dill, chopped
- 2 tablespoons vegetable oil
- 2 tablespoons butter
- 1 teaspoon saffron threads (soaked in warm water)
- 1 tablespoon yogurt
- Salt and pepper to taste

Optional Garnish:

- Sliced almonds or pistachios

Instructions:

Prepare the Chicken:
- In a large pot, sauté finely chopped onions in vegetable oil until golden brown.
- Add turmeric, salt, and pepper. Stir well.
- Add chicken pieces to the pot and brown them on all sides.
- Pour in water, cover the pot, and let the chicken cook until tender.

Cook the Rice:

- Rinse Basmati rice under cold water until the water runs clear.
- In a separate pot, bring 4 cups of water to a boil. Add salt and rice to the boiling water.
- Cook the rice until it's parboiled (partially cooked) and still has a bite to it. Drain the rice.

Prepare the Baghali Polo:
- In a pan, sauté frozen lima beans in vegetable oil until they are cooked.
- Add chopped dill to the lima beans and mix well.
- In a large pot, melt butter. Add a layer of parboiled rice, followed by a layer of the lima bean and dill mixture. Repeat the layers until both rice and lima beans are used up.
- Dissolve saffron in warm water and mix it with yogurt. Drizzle this saffron-infused yogurt mixture over the top layer of rice.

Steam the Rice:
- Cover the pot with a clean kitchen towel and a tight-fitting lid. Cook on low heat for about 1 to 1.5 hours to allow the rice to steam and fully cook.

Serve:
- Once the Baghali Polo Ba Morgh is ready, gently fluff the rice with a fork.
- Serve the chicken pieces on top of the rice, and garnish with sliced almonds or pistachios if desired.

Enjoy:
- Baghali Polo Ba Morgh is ready to be enjoyed. It's a flavorful and aromatic dish that combines the richness of chicken with the freshness of dill and lima beans.

This Persian dish is a celebration of aromatic herbs and the perfect blend of flavors. The dill and lima beans add a unique and delightful touch to the rice, making it a favorite among Persian culinary traditions.

Tahdig (Crispy Rice)

Ingredients:

- 2 cups Basmati rice
- 4 cups water
- 3 tablespoons vegetable oil or butter
- Salt to taste

Instructions:

Rinse the Rice:
- Rinse the Basmati rice under cold water until the water runs clear. This helps remove excess starch.

Parboil the Rice:
- In a large pot, bring 4 cups of water to a boil. Add salt to the boiling water.
- Add the rinsed rice to the boiling water and cook until the rice is parboiled (partially cooked), still having a bite to it. The rice grains should be firm.
- Drain the parboiled rice in a colander and set it aside.

Create a Layer of Oil or Butter:
- In the same pot, add vegetable oil or butter and spread it across the bottom evenly. The layer should be thick enough to prevent the rice from sticking.

Layer the Parboiled Rice:
- Return the parboiled rice to the pot, creating an even layer on top of the oil or butter.

Create Steam Holes:
- Using the back of a spoon or the handle of a spatula, poke several holes in the rice, reaching down to the bottom. This allows steam to escape and helps form the crispy layer.

Steam and Crisp:
- Cover the pot with a clean kitchen towel and a tight-fitting lid. Cook on low heat for about 30 to 45 minutes. The low heat allows the Tahdig to slowly crisp up without burning.
- Check periodically to ensure the bottom is turning golden brown. Adjust the heat if needed.

Invert the Tahdig:
- Once the Tahdig is golden and crispy, remove the pot from heat. Place a large plate or a flat serving platter over the pot.

- Holding the pot and the plate securely together, carefully invert the pot so that the Tahdig is now on top.

Serve:
- The crispy Tahdig is ready to be served. Cut it into wedges or squares and serve it alongside your main dish.

Enjoy:
- Tahdig is a delicious and prized element of Persian cuisine. Its crispy texture and flavorful taste make it a highlight of any meal.

Tahdig is often served with various Persian stews and dishes, adding a delightful crunch to the meal. It's a culinary tradition that showcases the artistry of Persian rice cooking.

Khoresh-e Gheymeh Bademjan (Eggplant and Meat Stew)
Ingredients:

- 1 pound (about 500g) lamb or beef, cut into cubes
- 2 large eggplants, peeled and cubed
- 1 cup yellow split peas, soaked
- 2 onions, finely chopped
- 3 tablespoons tomato paste
- 1 teaspoon turmeric
- Salt and pepper to taste
- Vegetable oil for frying
- 2-3 dried limes (limoo amani), pierced
- 1 tablespoon dried fenugreek leaves (optional)
- 1 tablespoon dried lime powder (optional, for additional tanginess)
- 2 tablespoons lime or lemon juice
- 2 tablespoons sugar (optional, for balancing flavors)
- Cooked rice for serving

Instructions:

Prepare Yellow Split Peas:
- Soak yellow split peas in water for a few hours or overnight. Drain before using.

Fry the Eggplants:
- In a deep pan, heat vegetable oil over medium heat. Fry the cubed eggplants until golden brown. Remove and set aside on paper towels to drain excess oil.

Brown the Meat:
- In the same pan, brown the meat cubes on all sides. Add chopped onions and sauté until onions are golden.

Cook Yellow Split Peas:
- Add soaked and drained yellow split peas to the meat and onions. Stir well.

Add Tomato Paste and Spices:
- Stir in tomato paste, turmeric, salt, and pepper. Mix thoroughly.

Add Dried Limes:
- Pierce the dried limes (limoo amani) and add them to the pot for flavor. If using dried lime powder, add it at this point.

Simmer:
- Pour enough water to cover the ingredients. Bring the stew to a boil, then reduce the heat to low, cover the pot, and let it simmer for about 1.5 to 2 hours or until the meat is tender.

Add Eggplants and Fenugreek:
- Add the fried eggplants to the stew. If using dried fenugreek leaves, add them as well. Mix gently.

Adjust Seasoning:
- Taste the stew and adjust the seasoning. Add lime or lemon juice for acidity. If desired, add sugar to balance flavors.

Continue Simmering:
- Let the stew simmer for an additional 30 minutes to allow the flavors to meld.

Serve:
- Khoresh-e Gheymeh Bademjan is ready to be served. Remove the dried limes before serving.

Enjoy:
- Serve the stew over a bed of cooked rice. It's a hearty and flavorful dish that showcases the rich combination of meat, eggplants, and aromatic spices.

Khoresh-e Gheymeh Bademjan is a comforting and savory stew that is enjoyed in Persian cuisine. The combination of eggplants, meat, and yellow split peas creates a rich and satisfying dish.

Havij Polo (Carrot Rice)

Ingredients:

- 2 cups Basmati rice
- 4 cups water
- 3 cups carrots, julienned or grated
- 1 large onion, finely chopped
- 1/4 cup vegetable oil or butter
- 1/2 teaspoon ground cinnamon
- Salt and pepper to taste
- 1/2 cup slivered almonds or chopped pistachios (optional, for garnish)

Instructions:

Rinse the Rice:
- Rinse the Basmati rice under cold water until the water runs clear. This helps remove excess starch.

Sauté Onions:
- In a pot, heat vegetable oil or butter over medium heat. Sauté the finely chopped onion until it becomes golden brown.

Add Carrots:
- Add the julienned or grated carrots to the pot. Sauté the carrots until they are slightly tender but still have a crunch.

Add Spices:
- Sprinkle ground cinnamon over the carrots and onions. Season with salt and pepper to taste. Mix well to coat the carrots in the spices.

Cook Rice:
- Add the rinsed Basmati rice to the pot, stirring gently to combine with the carrots and onions.
- Pour in 4 cups of water and bring it to a boil. Reduce the heat to low, cover the pot with a tight-fitting lid, and let the rice simmer until it's fully cooked.

Fluff the Rice:
- Once the rice is cooked, use a fork to fluff it gently. Be careful not to mash the rice grains.

Optional Garnish:
- If desired, garnish the Havij Polo with slivered almonds or chopped pistachios.

Serve:

- Havij Polo is ready to be served. It can be served as a side dish or as a main course.

Enjoy:
- Enjoy the sweet and aromatic flavors of Havij Polo. It pairs well with a variety of Persian stews and dishes.

Havij Polo is a vibrant and flavorful dish that adds a touch of sweetness to your meal. The combination of carrots, spices, and perfectly cooked rice creates a delightful and visually appealing dish in Persian cuisine.

Koofteh Sabzi (Herb Meatballs)

Ingredients:

For the Meatballs:

- 1 pound ground beef or lamb
- 1 cup cooked rice
- 1 cup mixed fresh herbs (parsley, cilantro, dill, and green onions), finely chopped
- 1 large onion, grated
- 2 cloves garlic, minced
- 1/2 cup chickpea flour (besan) or breadcrumbs
- 1 teaspoon ground turmeric
- Salt and pepper to taste

For the Filling (Optional):

- Hard-boiled eggs, peeled
- Dried fruits (apricots, prunes, or barberries)

For the Sauce:

- 2 onions, finely chopped
- 2 tablespoons tomato paste
- 1 teaspoon ground turmeric
- 1/2 cup mixed fresh herbs, finely chopped
- Vegetable oil for cooking
- Salt and pepper to taste

Instructions:

Prepare the Meatball Mixture:
- In a large mixing bowl, combine ground meat, cooked rice, finely chopped fresh herbs, grated onion, minced garlic, chickpea flour (or breadcrumbs), ground turmeric, salt, and pepper.

Mix Thoroughly:
- Use your hands to mix the ingredients thoroughly until well combined. The mixture should have a cohesive and slightly sticky texture.

Prepare the Filling (Optional):

- If using a filling, take a small portion of the meatball mixture and flatten it in your hand. Place a piece of hard-boiled egg or a small amount of dried fruit in the center, then encase it with the meat mixture, forming a ball.

Shape the Meatballs:
- Wet your hands with cold water to prevent sticking, then shape the meat mixture into large meatballs. If using a filling, make sure it's fully enclosed within each meatball.

Prepare the Sauce:
- In a separate pan, sauté finely chopped onions in vegetable oil until golden brown.
- Add tomato paste, ground turmeric, and chopped fresh herbs. Cook for a few minutes until the herbs are fragrant.
- Season the sauce with salt and pepper to taste.

Cook the Meatballs:
- In a large pot, heat vegetable oil. Brown the meatballs on all sides.
- Once browned, add the prepared sauce to the pot, covering the meatballs.

Simmer:
- Reduce the heat to low, cover the pot, and let the meatballs simmer in the sauce for about 45 minutes to 1 hour. Ensure the meatballs are fully cooked.

Serve:
- Koofteh Sabzi is ready to be served. Serve it with rice or flatbread.

Enjoy:
- Koofteh Sabzi is a flavorful and aromatic dish with the freshness of herbs complementing the savory meatballs. It's a delightful addition to Persian cuisine.

Feel free to customize the recipe based on your preferences, and enjoy the unique blend of herbs and spices in Koofteh Sabzi!

Khoresht-e Beh (Quince Stew)

Ingredients:

- 1 pound (about 500g) meat (lamb or beef), cubed
- 2 large quinces, peeled, cored, and sliced
- 1 large onion, finely chopped
- 3 tablespoons vegetable oil
- 2 tablespoons tomato paste
- 1 teaspoon ground turmeric
- 1 teaspoon ground cinnamon
- Salt and pepper to taste
- 1 cup water or beef broth
- 2 tablespoons sugar (adjust to taste)
- 2 tablespoons lime or lemon juice (adjust to taste)
- Saffron threads (optional, soaked in warm water)
- Cooked rice for serving

Instructions:

Sauté Onions:
- In a pot, heat vegetable oil over medium heat. Sauté chopped onions until golden brown.

Brown the Meat:
- Add the cubed meat to the pot. Brown the meat on all sides to seal in the flavors.

Add Spices:
- Stir in ground turmeric, ground cinnamon, salt, and pepper. Mix well to coat the meat with the spices.

Add Tomato Paste:
- Add tomato paste to the pot and continue stirring for a couple of minutes to incorporate it into the mixture.

Pour Water or Broth:
- Pour water or beef broth into the pot, ensuring that the ingredients are fully covered.

Simmer:
- Bring the stew to a boil, then reduce the heat to low, cover the pot, and let it simmer for about 1.5 to 2 hours or until the meat is tender and the flavors meld.

Prepare Quinces:
- While the stew is simmering, peel, core, and slice the quinces.

Add Quinces to the Stew:
- Add the sliced quinces to the pot. If using saffron, add the saffron-infused water at this point.

Sweeten and Acidify:
- Add sugar to the stew, adjusting the sweetness to your liking. Similarly, add lime or lemon juice for acidity, adjusting to taste.

Continue Simmering:
- Let the stew continue to simmer until the quinces are tender and the flavors have melded.

Adjust Seasoning:
- Taste the stew and adjust the seasoning, sugar, or acidity if needed.

Serve:
- Khoresht-e Beh is ready to be served. Serve it over a bed of cooked rice.

Enjoy:
- Enjoy the unique combination of savory meat, sweet quinces, and aromatic spices in this Persian quince stew.

Khoresht-e Beh is a delightful dish that showcases the sweet and tangy flavor of quinces combined with savory elements. It's a wonderful addition to Persian cuisine.

Zaban (Persian Beef Tongue Stew)
Ingredients:

- 1 beef tongue, thoroughly cleaned
- 1 large onion, finely chopped
- 3 tablespoons vegetable oil
- 2 tablespoons tomato paste
- 1 teaspoon ground turmeric
- 1 teaspoon ground cinnamon
- 1 teaspoon ground cumin
- Salt and pepper to taste
- 4 cups water or beef broth
- 2 tablespoons lime or lemon juice
- 2 tablespoons pomegranate molasses (optional, for a tangy flavor)
- 1 tablespoon sugar (optional)
- Fresh herbs for garnish (parsley, cilantro, or mint)
- Cooked rice or flatbread for serving

Instructions:

Prepare the Beef Tongue:
- Thoroughly clean the beef tongue, removing any excess fat or membrane.

Boil the Beef Tongue:
- Place the cleaned beef tongue in a pot, cover it with water, and bring it to a boil. Let it simmer for about 10-15 minutes.
- Drain the water and rinse the tongue under cold water. This process helps remove any impurities.

Cook the Beef Tongue:
- In a clean pot, heat vegetable oil over medium heat. Sauté chopped onions until golden brown.
- Add ground turmeric, ground cinnamon, ground cumin, salt, and pepper. Mix well.
- Add the boiled beef tongue to the pot. Brown the tongue on all sides.

Add Tomato Paste:
- Stir in tomato paste and continue cooking for a few minutes to incorporate it into the mixture.

Pour Water or Broth:
- Pour water or beef broth into the pot, ensuring that the tongue is fully covered.

Simmer:
- Bring the stew to a boil, then reduce the heat to low, cover the pot, and let it simmer for about 2-3 hours or until the beef tongue is tender.

Slice the Beef Tongue:
- Once the beef tongue is tender, remove it from the pot and let it cool slightly. Slice the tongue into thin slices.

Prepare the Sauce:
- In the pot, add lime or lemon juice, pomegranate molasses (if using), and sugar (if using). Adjust the seasoning to your liking.

Combine Tongue and Sauce:
- Return the sliced beef tongue to the pot, ensuring it's coated with the flavorful sauce.

Simmer Again:
- Let the stew simmer for an additional 15-20 minutes to allow the flavors to meld.

Garnish and Serve:
- Garnish the Zaban with fresh herbs. It's now ready to be served.

Enjoy:
- Serve Zaban over a bed of cooked rice or with flatbread. The tender beef tongue and flavorful sauce make for a unique and delicious dish.

Zaban is a distinctive and savory dish that showcases the use of beef tongue in Persian cuisine. The combination of spices and optional tangy ingredients creates a rich and flavorful stew.

Sholeh Zard (Saffron Rice Pudding)

Ingredients:

- 1 cup Basmati rice
- 4 cups water
- 2 cups sugar
- 1/2 cup unsalted butter
- 1/2 teaspoon ground saffron threads (soaked in warm water)
- 1/4 teaspoon ground cinnamon
- 1/4 cup slivered almonds (for garnish)
- 1/4 cup slivered pistachios (for garnish)
- 1/4 cup slivered or shredded coconut (for garnish)
- Ground cinnamon for sprinkling (optional)

Instructions:

Rinse and Soak Rice:
- Rinse Basmati rice under cold water until the water runs clear. Soak the rice in water for at least 2 hours.

Cook the Rice:
- In a large pot, bring 4 cups of water to a boil. Drain the soaked rice and add it to the boiling water. Cook the rice until it's soft but still has a bit of bite to it. Drain the rice.

Prepare Saffron:
- Soak ground saffron threads in a small amount of warm water and set aside to infuse.

Make Sugar Syrup:
- In a separate pot, combine sugar with 2 cups of water. Bring it to a boil, stirring until the sugar is fully dissolved. Simmer for a few minutes to create a sugar syrup.

Combine Rice and Sugar Syrup:
- Add the drained rice to the sugar syrup. Stir well and let it simmer over low heat. The rice will absorb the sugar syrup and become fragrant.

Add Saffron and Butter:
- Add the saffron-infused water and unsalted butter to the rice mixture. Mix well to combine.

Simmer:

- Let the mixture simmer over low heat, stirring occasionally, until it reaches a pudding-like consistency. This may take about 30-40 minutes.

Serve:
- Sholeh Zard is traditionally served in flat dishes or shallow bowls. Smooth the surface with a spatula or spoon.

Garnish:
- Garnish the Sholeh Zard with slivered almonds, slivered pistachios, and shredded coconut. Optionally, sprinkle ground cinnamon on top.

Chill:
- Let the Sholeh Zard cool to room temperature, then refrigerate for a few hours or overnight. This allows the flavors to meld.

Enjoy:
- Sholeh Zard is ready to be enjoyed. Serve it chilled and savor the fragrant saffron-infused rice pudding.

Sholeh Zard is not only delicious but also a visually appealing dessert with its vibrant saffron color and nutty garnishes. It's a classic treat in Persian cuisine, often served during celebrations and festive gatherings.

Kalam Polo Ba Morgh (Cabbage Rice with Chicken)
Ingredients:

For the Chicken:

- 1 whole chicken, cut into pieces
- 1 large onion, finely chopped
- 3 tablespoons vegetable oil
- 1 teaspoon ground turmeric
- Salt and pepper to taste
- Water for boiling

For the Cabbage and Rice:

- 1 medium-sized cabbage, shredded
- 2 cups Basmati rice, rinsed and soaked
- 1 large onion, finely chopped
- 3 tablespoons vegetable oil
- 1 teaspoon ground turmeric
- Salt and pepper to taste

For the Tomato Sauce:

- 2 large tomatoes, grated or finely chopped
- 2 tablespoons tomato paste
- 1 teaspoon ground cinnamon
- Salt and pepper to taste

Optional Garnish:

- Slivered almonds or pistachios

Instructions:

Prepare Chicken:
- In a pot, heat vegetable oil over medium heat. Sauté chopped onions until golden brown.
- Add chicken pieces, ground turmeric, salt, and pepper. Brown the chicken on all sides.

- Add enough water to the pot to cover the chicken. Bring it to a boil, then reduce the heat, cover the pot, and let the chicken simmer until fully cooked. Once cooked, remove the chicken from the broth and set aside.

Cook Cabbage and Rice:
- In a separate pot, heat vegetable oil over medium heat. Sauté chopped onions until golden brown.
- Add shredded cabbage to the pot and cook until softened.
- Drain the soaked Basmati rice and add it to the pot. Mix well with the cabbage.
- Season with ground turmeric, salt, and pepper. Stir to combine.

Prepare Tomato Sauce:
- In a bowl, mix grated or finely chopped tomatoes with tomato paste, ground cinnamon, salt, and pepper.
- Pour the tomato sauce over the cabbage and rice mixture. Mix gently to evenly distribute the sauce.

Layer Chicken and Cabbage-Rice Mixture:
- In a large pot, create a layer of the cabbage and rice mixture. Place the cooked chicken pieces on top.
- Repeat the layers until all the ingredients are used, finishing with a layer of the cabbage and rice mixture on top.

Steam:
- Cover the pot with a clean kitchen towel and a tight-fitting lid. Cook on low heat for about 1 to 1.5 hours to allow the rice to steam and fully cook.

Garnish (Optional):
- If desired, garnish the Kalam Polo Ba Morgh with slivered almonds or pistachios.

Serve:
- Once the dish is fully cooked and the rice is tender, gently fluff the rice with a fork.
- Serve Kalam Polo Ba Morgh on a platter, ensuring to include layers of both the cabbage and rice mixture and the chicken.

Enjoy:
- Kalam Polo Ba Morgh is ready to be enjoyed. The combination of cabbage, rice, and flavorful chicken creates a hearty and delicious dish.

This Persian dish is a celebration of flavors and textures, making it a delightful addition to your culinary repertoire.

Gondi Polo (Chickpea and Chicken Rice)

Ingredients:

For the Chicken:

- 1 whole chicken, cut into pieces
- 1 large onion, finely chopped
- 3 tablespoons vegetable oil
- 1 teaspoon ground turmeric
- Salt and pepper to taste
- Water for boiling

For the Chickpeas:

- 1 cup dried chickpeas, soaked overnight (or canned chickpeas)
- 1 teaspoon baking soda (if using dried chickpeas)
- Water for boiling
- Salt to taste

For the Rice:

- 2 cups Basmati rice, rinsed and soaked
- 1 large onion, thinly sliced
- 3 tablespoons vegetable oil
- 1 teaspoon ground turmeric
- Salt and pepper to taste

For the Garnish:

- Slivered almonds or pistachios
- Dried barberries (zereshk), soaked in water (optional)
- Saffron threads, soaked in warm water (optional)

Instructions:

Prepare Chicken:
- In a pot, heat vegetable oil over medium heat. Sauté chopped onions until golden brown.
- Add chicken pieces, ground turmeric, salt, and pepper. Brown the chicken on all sides.

- Add enough water to the pot to cover the chicken. Bring it to a boil, then reduce the heat, cover the pot, and let the chicken simmer until fully cooked. Once cooked, remove the chicken from the broth and set aside.

Prepare Chickpeas:
- If using dried chickpeas, drain and rinse them. Place them in a pot, cover with water, add baking soda, and bring to a boil. Cook until chickpeas are tender. If using canned chickpeas, drain and rinse them.
- Season the cooked chickpeas with salt and set aside.

Cook Rice:
- In a separate pot, heat vegetable oil over medium heat. Sauté thinly sliced onions until golden brown.
- Drain the soaked Basmati rice and add it to the pot. Mix well with the sautéed onions.
- Season with ground turmeric, salt, and pepper. Stir to combine.

Layer Chicken, Chickpeas, and Rice:
- In a large pot, create layers of rice, cooked chicken pieces, and chickpeas. Repeat until all ingredients are used, finishing with a layer of rice on top.

Steam:
- Cover the pot with a clean kitchen towel and a tight-fitting lid. Cook on low heat for about 1 to 1.5 hours to allow the rice to steam and fully cook.

Garnish:
- If desired, garnish the Gondi Polo with slivered almonds or pistachios, drained barberries, and saffron-infused water.

Serve:
- Once the dish is fully cooked and the rice is tender, gently fluff the rice with a fork.
- Serve Gondi Polo on a platter, ensuring to include layers of both the rice and the chicken-chickpea mixture.

Enjoy:
- Gondi Polo is ready to be enjoyed. The combination of chickpeas, chicken, and fragrant rice makes for a flavorful and satisfying dish.

Gondi Polo is a festive dish often prepared for special occasions, offering a delightful blend of textures and tastes.

Reshteh Polo (Rice with Noodles and Herbs)

Ingredients:

For the Rice:

- 2 cups Basmati rice, rinsed and soaked
- 1/2 cup vegetable oil or ghee
- 1 teaspoon ground saffron threads (soaked in warm water)
- Salt and pepper to taste

For the Noodles and Herbs:

- 1 cup reshteh (thin noodles), broken into small pieces
- 1 cup chopped fresh herbs (a mix of parsley, cilantro, and dill)
- 1 large onion, finely chopped
- 3 tablespoons vegetable oil
- 1 teaspoon ground turmeric
- Salt and pepper to taste

Optional Garnish:

- Slivered almonds or pistachios

Instructions:

Cook the Rice:
- In a pot, bring water to a boil. Add salt and the soaked Basmati rice. Cook until the rice is parboiled (half-cooked). Drain the rice.
- In the same pot, heat vegetable oil or ghee. Place a layer of parboiled rice at the bottom, sprinkle saffron water on top, and repeat until all the rice is used. Cover the pot with a clean kitchen towel and a tight-fitting lid. Cook on low heat for about 1 to 1.5 hours to allow the rice to steam and fully cook.

Prepare Noodles and Herbs:
- In a separate pan, heat vegetable oil over medium heat. Sauté chopped onions until golden brown.
- Add broken reshteh (noodles) to the pan. Stir and cook until the noodles are golden.
- Add ground turmeric, salt, and pepper. Mix well.

- Stir in the chopped fresh herbs and cook until they are wilted.

Layer Rice and Noodles-Herbs Mixture:
- Once both the rice and the noodle-herb mixture are ready, create layers in a serving dish. Start with a layer of rice, followed by a layer of the noodle-herb mixture. Repeat until all ingredients are used.

Garnish (Optional):
- If desired, garnish the Reshteh Polo with slivered almonds or pistachios.

Serve:
- Once the dish is fully assembled, gently fluff the rice and mix it with the noodle-herb layers.
- Serve Reshteh Polo on a platter, ensuring to include both the rice and the noodle-herb layers in each serving.

Enjoy:
- Reshteh Polo is ready to be enjoyed. The combination of fluffy rice, saffron, and the flavorful noodle-herb mixture makes for a delightful meal.

Reshteh Polo is a classic Persian dish that offers a unique combination of textures and flavors, making it a wonderful addition to a Persian lunch spread.

Reshteh Polo (Rice with Noodles and Herbs)
Ingredients:

For the Rice:

- 2 cups Basmati rice, rinsed and soaked
- 1/2 cup vegetable oil or ghee
- 1 teaspoon ground saffron threads (soaked in warm water)
- Salt and pepper to taste

For the Noodles and Herbs:

- 1 cup reshteh (thin noodles), broken into small pieces
- 1 cup chopped fresh herbs (a mix of parsley, cilantro, and dill)
- 1 large onion, finely chopped
- 3 tablespoons vegetable oil
- 1 teaspoon ground turmeric
- Salt and pepper to taste

Optional Garnish:

- Slivered almonds or pistachios

Instructions:

Cook the Rice:
- In a pot, bring water to a boil. Add salt and the soaked Basmati rice. Cook until the rice is parboiled (half-cooked). Drain the rice.
- In the same pot, heat vegetable oil or ghee. Place a layer of parboiled rice at the bottom, sprinkle saffron water on top, and repeat until all the rice is used. Cover the pot with a clean kitchen towel and a tight-fitting lid. Cook on low heat for about 1 to 1.5 hours to allow the rice to steam and fully cook.

Prepare Noodles and Herbs:
- In a separate pan, heat vegetable oil over medium heat. Sauté chopped onions until golden brown.
- Add broken reshteh (noodles) to the pan. Stir and cook until the noodles are golden.
- Add ground turmeric, salt, and pepper. Mix well.
- Stir in the chopped fresh herbs and cook until they are wilted.

Layer Rice and Noodles-Herbs Mixture:
- Once both the rice and the noodle-herb mixture are ready, create layers in a serving dish. Start with a layer of rice, followed by a layer of the noodle-herb mixture. Repeat until all ingredients are used.

Garnish (Optional):
- If desired, garnish the Reshteh Polo with slivered almonds or pistachios.

Serve:
- Once the dish is fully assembled, gently fluff the rice and mix it with the noodle-herb layers.
- Serve Reshteh Polo on a platter, ensuring to include both the rice and the noodle-herb layers in each serving.

Enjoy:
- Reshteh Polo is ready to be enjoyed. The combination of fluffy rice, saffron, and the flavorful noodle-herb mixture makes for a delightful meal.

Reshteh Polo is a classic Persian dish that offers a unique combination of textures and flavors, making it a wonderful addition to a Persian lunch spread.

www.ingramcontent.com/pod-product-compliance
Lightning Source LLC
LaVergne TN
LVHW081610060526
838201LV00054B/2182